Letts
gets you through

C000005253

KS2 MATHS
SATs SUCCESS
10–MINUTE TESTS

Ages 10–11

KS2 MATHS SATs

10–MINUTE TESTS

JASON WHITE

Sample page

clear instructional text   topic being covered   test number for quick reference

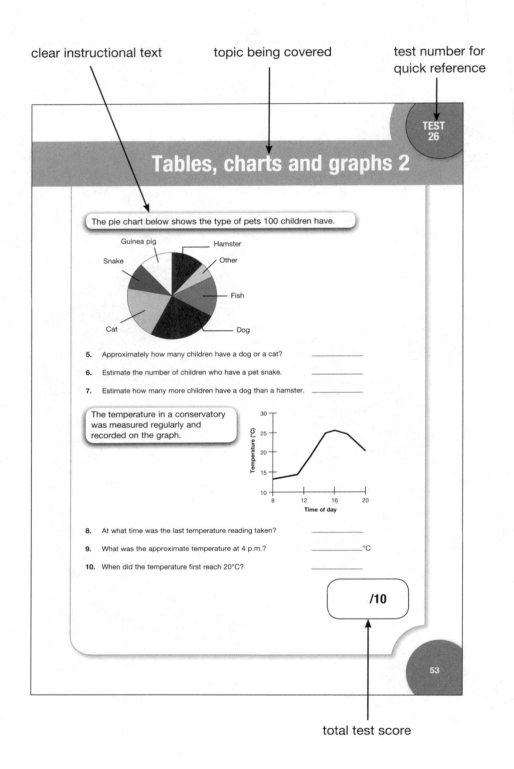

TEST 26

Tables, charts and graphs 2

The pie chart below shows the type of pets 100 children have.

Guinea pig   Hamster
Snake   Other
Fish
Cat   Dog

5. Approximately how many children have a dog or a cat?   _____

6. Estimate the number of children who have a pet snake.   _____

7. Estimate how many more children have a dog than a hamster.   _____

The temperature in a conservatory was measured regularly and recorded on the graph.

(graph: Temperature (°C) vs Time of day, axis from 10 to 30, time from 8 to 20)

8. At what time was the last temperature reading taken?   _____

9. What was the approximate temperature at 4 p.m.?   _____°C

10. When did the temperature first reach 20°C?   _____

/10

53

total test score

Contents

Place value and ordering

1. Put a circle around the largest number below.

   10 358   10 538   10 835   10 700   10 799

2. Write in words the value of the digit in bold in each number.

   a) 1**2**89   _____

   b) 12**2**89   _____

   c) 128**9**52   _____

3. Calculate the following.

   a) 1327 + 72 + 154 =   _____

   b) 549 + 91 + 3584 =   _____

   c) 2057 + 1424 + 49 =   _____

4. Put these numbers in order, starting with the **smallest**.

   a) 2851   1067   2809   2799   4001

   b) 6430   6515   7000   6001   6099

5. Put these numbers in order, starting with the **largest**.

   a) 12 483   103 826   17 001   1 031 710   87 271

   b) 4 280 338   583 200   2 984 988   560 200   100 999

6. Put these decimals in order, starting with the **smallest**.

   a) 4.2   4.03   4.27   4.09   4.099

   b) 20.9   20.72   24.27   20.01   24.4

Place value and ordering

7. Put these fractions in order, starting with the **largest**.

$\frac{7}{3}$ $\frac{12}{5}$ $\frac{7}{2}$ $\frac{10}{9}$ $\frac{3}{2}$

8. Six boys from class 4 have their height measured.

Jon
1.38 m

Eric
1.19 m

Ahmed
1.4 m

Jake
1.09 m

George
1.2 m

Billy
1.41 m

a) Who is the tallest boy? _____

b) Who is the second smallest boy? _____

c) Who is the third tallest boy? _____

9. The cost of five train journeys is as follows:

A   Nottingham – Lincoln   £10   B   Macclesfield – Stoke   £8.50

C   Carlisle – Manchester   £13.29   D   London – Bristol   £24

E   Brighton – London   £16.90

a) Write the letter of the cheapest journey.   _____

b) Write the letter of the second least expensive journey.   _____

c) Write the letter of the most expensive journey.   _____

10. The total minutes played by a football team's players during a season was as follows.

Player	Minutes played
Johnson	3784
Smith	2072
Adams	4365
Grant	1309
Morgan	1091

a) Which player played the second fewest number of minutes? _____

b) Which player played the third most number of minutes?

_____

/10

Rounding and approximating

1. Round each of these numbers to the **nearest 10**.

    a)   435   367   901   251

    b)   6478   7045   8889   5807

    c)   29 837   17 995   21 001   99 507

2. Round each of these numbers to the **nearest 100**.

    a)   239   965   687   309

    b)   5809   4150   6668   3359

    c)   23 059   57 868   30 951   89 982

    d)   128 308   451 222   927 010   369 971

3. Round each of these numbers to the **nearest 1000**.

    a)   560   2506   6444   8099

    b)   11 555   29 537   68 299   37 085

    c)   222 481   708 564   501 901   199 489

4. Here are the heights of six children.
    Round each child's height to the nearest 10 cm.

| Child 1 | Child 2 | Child 3 | Child 4 | Child 5 | Child 6 |
| 1.24 m | 1.31 m | 1.2 m | 1.41 m | 1.33 m | 1.49 m |

Child 1 = _____ m   Child 2 = _____ m   Child 3 = _____ m

Child 4 = _____ m   Child 5 = _____ m   Child 6 = _____ m

Rounding and approximating

5. Estimate the answers to the questions below and then check your answers with a calculator.

Question	Estimate	Answer
2129 + 3454		
24 783 + 15 031		
7.92 + 15.01		
5203 − 3487		

6. Estimate how much water is in this jug.

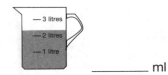

_____ ml

7. Look at these scales and estimate the weight.

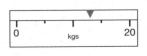

_____ kg

8. The boy shown is 123 cm tall. Estimate the height of the woman standing next to him.

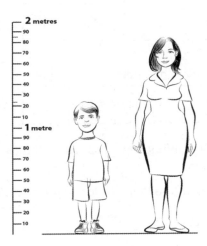

_____ cm

9. Lily can read two pages in her reading book in 4 minutes and 6 seconds. Approximately how long will it take Lily to read 30 pages?

_____ minutes

10. Approximately how many weeks are there in 50 years?

_____ weeks

/10

Number patterns and negative numbers

1. Work out the next two numbers in this sequence.

| 3 | 6 | 12 | 24 | | |

2. Work out the next two numbers in this sequence.

| 160 | 80 | 40 | 20 | | |

3. Draw the next two shapes in this sequence.

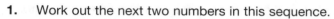

4. Work out the missing number in this sequence.

| −14 | −8 | | 4 | 10 | 16 |

5. Work out the missing numbers in this sequence.

| 13 | 5 | | −11 | −19 | |

6. The temperature in a fridge is −4°C. When the electricity is turned off, the temperature rises by 3°C every hour.

   What is the temperature in the fridge four hours after the electricity is turned off?

   _____°C

7. A liquid freezes at −16°C. The frozen liquid is heated up by 6°C every 30 minutes.

   What is the temperature of the liquid after two hours of heating?

   _____°C

Number patterns and negative numbers

8. Look at the thermometer.

If the temperature cooled by 18°C, what would be the new reading on the thermometer?

_____°C

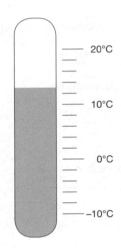

9. Look at the thermometer.

If the temperature increased by 14°C, what would be the new reading on the thermometer?

_____°C

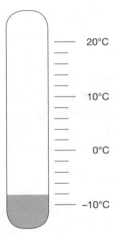

10. A thermometer reads 27°C. If the temperature drops by 3°C every two hours, how long would it take for the temperature to reach –9°C?

_____ hours

/10

Formulae and equations

1. Work out the value of q in the following equation.

   $215 - q = 148$ $q =$ _____

2. What is the value of z in the equation below?

   $z + 92 = 308$ $z =$ _____

3. $s + t + w = 112$

   If $s = 32$ and $t = w$, what is the value of w?

   $w =$ _____

4. There are 146 marbles in a jar. 18 are red, 28 are green and the rest are blue or yellow. There are three times more yellow than blue. Work out the number of blue marbles and the number of yellow marbles.

   Blue marbles = _____   Yellow marbles = _____

5. In a cinema there were 200 adults and children. If there was one adult for every three children, how many adults and how many children were there?

   Adults = _____

   Children = _____

6. **a)** If $36 - y = x$, what are all the possible values of x that are also a multiple of 4?

b) If $28 = zy$, what are all the pairs of whole numbers which satisfy this equation?

7. A rectangle has a perimeter of 54 cm. The lengths of the longest sides are double those of the shortest sides. What are the lengths of the sides?

Shortest = _____ cm

Longest = _____ cm

8. A boy is eight years older than his sister. How old is his sister when he is three times older than her?

_____

9. $a = 9$, $b = 2a$, $c = b - a$

What is the value of c if a is doubled? $c =$ _____

10. $66z = 11y$

If $z = 7$, what is the value of y? $y =$ _____

/10

Decimals

1. Put a circle around the largest decimal below.

   8.02   8.002   8.2   8.022   8.020

2. Write in words the value of the digit in bold in each number.

   a) 14.0**5** _____

   b) 14.**5** _____

   c) 14.00**5** _____

3. Double the following decimals.

   a) 0.3 _____

   b) 1.4 _____

   c) 3.82 _____

   d) 0.09 _____

4. Work out the answers to these calculations.

   a) 1.2 x 3 = _____

   b) 4.08 x 5 = _____

   c) 6.1 x 7 = _____

   d) 13.02 x 2 = _____

5. Work out the answers to these calculations.

   a) 3.8 – 2.2 = _____

   b) 4.9 + 6.3 = _____

   c) 18.09 – 4.2 = _____

   d) 23.6 + 14.23 = _____

6. Harry has a weekly shopping list. This week he decides to get two weeks' worth of shopping in one go. Write the new amounts Harry must get.

	Old amount	New amount
Carrots	1200 g	kg
Potatoes	2.5 kg	kg
Tomatoes	0.45 kg	kg
Onions	3	
Peas	300 g	kg

7. Class 3 did a sponsored walk. They split into six groups and the money they raised was as follows:

Group 1: £13.28   Group 2: £10.50   Group 3: 1571p

Group 4: £8   Group 5: 1108p   Group 6: £12.99

How much money did class 3 raise altogether?   £ _____

8. Here are the weights of some children. Work out how much they weigh altogether.

25.4 kg   28.72 kg   21.8 kg   30.02 kg   33.19 kg   24.5 kg   _____ kg

9. A jug can hold 2,200 ml of water. It takes 100 jugs of water to fill a tank.

How much water can the tank hold if it is full? Give your answer in litres.

_____ litres

10. Mary measures her stride. It is 85 cm.

If Mary takes 200 strides, how many metres has she gone?

_____ m

/10

Addition

1. Calculate the answer to the following additions. Write the answers as numbers.

   a) Thirteen add fifty-eight = _____

   b) Seventy-five add thirty-four = _____

   c) Forty-six add ninety-seven = _____

2. Add these numbers.

   a) 128 + 308 = _____

   b) 437 + 292 = _____

   c) 830 + 405 = _____

3. Now work these out.

   a) $\begin{array}{r} 45 \\ +61 \\ \hline \\ \hline \end{array}$ **b)** $\begin{array}{r} 83 \\ +39 \\ \hline \\ \hline \end{array}$ **c)** $\begin{array}{r} 72 \\ +29 \\ \hline \\ \hline \end{array}$

4. Calculate the additions below.

   a) $\begin{array}{r} 1\,583 \\ +8\,769 \\ \hline \\ \hline \end{array}$ **b)** $\begin{array}{r} 40\,147 \\ +\ 6\,954 \\ \hline \\ \hline \end{array}$ **c)** $\begin{array}{r} 28\,024 \\ +79\,867 \\ \hline \\ \hline \end{array}$

5. Add together 14 258, 92 001, 12 119, 85 357 and 48 080.

   _____

6. Bill goes to the cinema and spends £4.60 to watch a film. He also buys a bag of popcorn which costs £2.75. How much does Bill spend altogether?

   £ _____

7. Jenny goes shopping and buys a dress, a top and a pair of shoes.
Calculate how much money Jenny spends.

Dress	£14.90
Top	£9.99
Shoes	£54.50

£ _____

8. How many metres of painting does a groundsman have to complete to mark out all of the lines shown on this netball court?

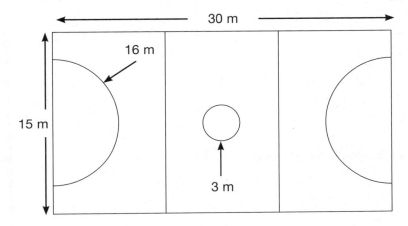

30 m

16 m

15 m

3 m

_____ m

9. How much money do these three children have altogether?

£ _____

£4.77

£8.43   £3.82

10. Write in the missing digits.

| 8 | | 9 | + | | 6 | 4 | = | 9 | 9 | 3 |

/10

Subtraction

1. Calculate the answer to the following subtractions. Write the answers as numbers.

   a) Seventy-three subtract twenty-seven = _____

   b) Ninety-four subtract thirty-six = _____

   c) Fifty-one subtract eighteen = _____

2. Calculate these subtractions.

   a) 571 – 358 = _____

   b) 907 – 668 = _____

   c) 325 – 179 = _____

3. Calculate the subtractions below.

   a)   82   b)   53   c)   61
        – 34   – 37   – 19
        ‾‾‾‾   ‾‾‾‾   ‾‾‾‾

        ‾‾‾‾   ‾‾‾‾   ‾‾‾‾

4. Find the answers to the following subtractions.

   a)   2508   b)   92 637   c)   700 312
        – 1793   – 24 081   – 92 743
        ‾‾‾‾‾   ‾‾‾‾‾‾   ‾‾‾‾‾‾‾

        ‾‾‾‾‾   ‾‾‾‾‾‾   ‾‾‾‾‾‾‾

5. Take away 265 096 from 1 062 884.

   _____

6. Heather has £20. She spends £12.27 in a shop.

   How much money does she have left?

   £ _____

Subtraction

7. Emily went shopping and spent £8.90 on food, £2.50 on some socks and £15 on a dress.

   How much money did she have left out of £30?

   £ _____

8. A baker had 6 kg of flour. He needed 225 g of flour to make one cake.

   If he made 12 cakes, how much flour did he have left?

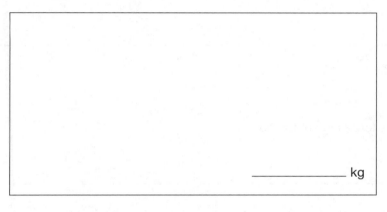

   _____ kg

9. A full tank holds 520 litres of water. The tank is then drained by pulling the plug out.

   40 litres of water drains through the plug hole every minute.

   How many minutes will it take until the tank holds 200 litres?

   _____ minutes

10. Write in the missing digits.

| 9 | 4 | | — | 3 | 9 | 8 | = | | 4 | 6 |

/10

Fractions

1. Calculate the answer to the following addition.

   $2\frac{5}{7} + 1\frac{4}{7} =$

2. Write in the missing fraction.

   $\frac{1}{8} + \frac{1}{4} + \boxed{} = 1$

3. Calculate the answer to the following subtraction.

   $5\frac{1}{6} - 3\frac{3}{4} =$

4. Calculate the answer to the following subtraction.

   $7\frac{2}{5} - 3\frac{7}{10} =$

5. Calculate the answer to the following multiplication.

   $\frac{2}{3} \times \frac{3}{4} =$

   Write the answer in its simplest form.

Fractions

6. Write the answers to the following divisions.

   a) $\frac{1}{3} \div 2 =$

   b) $\frac{3}{4} \div 6 =$

   c) $\frac{1}{4} \div 4 =$

7. Put the following fractions in order, starting with the **smallest**.

$$\frac{12}{3} \qquad \frac{19}{5} \qquad \frac{3}{2} \qquad \frac{29}{8} \qquad \frac{13}{6}$$

   _____   _____   _____   _____   _____

8. A survey was taken of 30 children's favourite flavour of ice cream. $\frac{2}{5}$ of the children liked strawberry, $\frac{1}{3}$ liked chocolate and the rest liked vanilla. What fraction of the children liked vanilla the best?

9. At a party, a birthday cake was divided into 24 equal pieces. $\frac{3}{8}$ of the cake was eaten straightaway and $\frac{1}{3}$ of the cake was taken home in party bags. What fraction of the cake was left?

10. Calculate $\frac{7}{3} + \frac{1}{4} + \frac{11}{12}$.

/10

Multiplication

1. Multiply the following numbers by 10, 100 and 1000.

    a) 2.71 x 10 = _____
        x 100 = _____
        x 1000 = _____

    b) 3.09 x 10 = _____
        x 100 = _____
        x 1000 = _____

    c) 46 x 10 = _____
        x 100 = _____
        x 1000 = _____

2. Calculate the answer to the following multiplication.

    ```
        1742
    x     23
    ```

3. Calculate the answer to the following multiplication.

    ```
        7061
    x     15
    ```

4. Calculate the answer to the following multiplication.

    ```
        5934
    x     61
    ```

5. An electrician earns £1732 every month. How much does she earn in a year?

6. Mr Morgan's newspaper bill is £11.57 each week. How much does Mr Morgan pay in a year?

7. In a box there are 36 watermelons. An average watermelon weighs 1250 g. Calculate the approximate total weight of watermelons in the box.

8. A rugby shirt costs £14.89. The rugby club need 19 shirts for their new team. How much will it cost to buy the 19 shirts?

9. Polly fills a bucket with water. She uses 43 cups of water altogether. Each cup holds 381 ml of water. How much water is there in the full bucket?

10. A fence panel is 1.245 m long. Mr Jones needs 23 panels to enclose his allotment. What is the perimeter of his allotment?

/10

Division

1. Divide the following numbers by 10, 100 and 1000.

   a) $24 \div 10 =$ _____
   $\div 100 =$ _____
   $\div 1000 =$ _____

   b) $357 \div 10 =$ _____
   $\div 100 =$ _____
   $\div 1000 =$ _____

   c) $2598 \div 10 =$ _____
   $\div 100 =$ _____
   $\div 1000 =$ _____

2. Work out the answer to the division below.

   $17 \overline{)1394}$

3. Work out the answer to the division below.

   $72 \overline{)2664}$

4. Work out the answer to the division below.

   $28 \overline{)2324}$

5. A plumber earns £2368 in July. He is paid £16 for every hour that he works. Calculate the number of hours he worked in July.

Division

6. Mrs Williams pays £1404 in a year for her electricity. How much does she need to save each week to pay her bill?

7. The weight of a tray of 36 eggs is 4.5 kg. What is the approximate weight of each egg?

8. The cost of a set of 14 football strips is £378. How much would just one strip cost?

9. Stanley fills a paddling pool with 18 buckets of water. This fills the paddling pool to its capacity of 288 litres. What is the capacity of the bucket?

10. The length of a roll of sticky tape is 10.37 m. A dispenser cuts pieces of 17 cm. How many pieces of sticky tape can be dispensed from each roll?

/10

Percentages

1. Write the following fractions as percentages.

   a) $\frac{1}{2}$ _____

   b) $\frac{1}{4}$ _____

   c) $\frac{3}{10}$ _____

   d) $\frac{3}{4}$ _____

2. Write the following decimals as percentages.

   a) 0.34 _____

   b) 0.57 _____

   c) 0.7 _____

   d) 0.03 _____

3. Write the following percentages as decimals.

   a) 49% _____

   b) 72% _____

   c) 5% _____

   d) 60% _____

4. What percentages of the grids below are shaded?

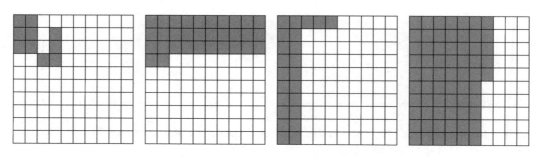

   a) _____%   b) _____%   c) _____%   d) _____%

Percentages

5. Calculate 50% of the following amounts.

    a)   42 kg   _____ kg

    b)   64 litres   _____ litres

    c)   3 km   _____ km

    d)   £70   £ _____

6. Calculate 30% of the following amounts.

    a)   £120   £ _____

    b)   200 m   _____ m

    c)   £4.00   £ _____

    d)   600 kg   _____ kg

7. There is a sale in a local game store. The sign says 25% off.

Tim buys a game that originally cost £24.

How much change does Tim get from £20?

£ _____

8. Sarah puts £300 in a bank account. The money earns 7% interest per year.

How much money does Sarah have in the account after one year's interest is added?

£ _____

9. A man who weighs 92 kg decides to go on a diet. He loses 10% of his weight.

What is his new weight?

_____ kg

10. A road is 800 km long. The length is increased by 25%.

How long is the road now?

_____ km

/10

Ratio and proportion

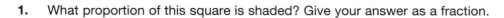

1. What proportion of this square is shaded? Give your answer as a fraction.

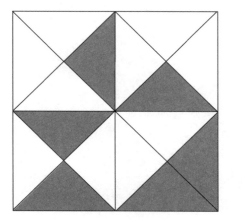

2. What proportion of this regular octagon is shaded? Give your answer as a fraction.

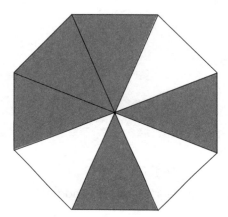

3. In a group of 10 children, four are boys and six are girls.
   What is the ratio of girls to boys?

   _____

4. There is a mixture of 14 red and yellow flowers in a bunch. The ratio of yellow to red is 6:1.
   What is the total number of yellow flowers in two bunches?

   _____

5. In a box of 40 marbles there are 24 black marbles and 16 white marbles.
   What is the ratio of black to white marbles?

   _____

Ratio and proportion

Look at the box of tiles shown.

6. What is the ratio of grey to white tiles?

_____

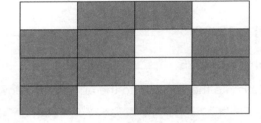

7. What proportion of the tiles are white?
Give your answer as a fraction.

8. In a group of 18 children, the ratio of boys to girls is 1:1.
How many boys and how many girls are there in the group?

Boys = _____

Girls = _____

9. Kelly has a birthday party. The ratio of children to adults is 4:1.
There are 24 children at the party. How many adults are there?

_____

10. Look at the cups of coffee on the tray.

What is the ratio of black to white cups?

_____

/10

Mixed 1

1. Write in words the value of the digit in bold in each number.

    a) 361**0**28 _____

    b) 2**5**27 815 _____

    c) **8**100 325 _____

2. Estimate the answers to the questions below and then check your answers with a calculator.

Question	Estimate	Answer
6138 + 8432		
36 867 + 13 014		
4.97 + 18.01		
8211 – 7501		

3. Work out the value of y in the following equation.

    157 – y = 88 y = _____

4. Write in the missing fraction.

    $\frac{3}{9}$ + $\frac{1}{6}$ + ☐ = 1

5. Here are the weights of some children. Work out how much they weigh altogether.

31.6 kg   27.38 kg   29.18 kg   31.07 kg   36.66 kg   27.5 kg

_____ kg

Mixed 1

6. Add these numbers.

   a) 516 + 157 = _____

   b) 347 + 611 = _____

   c) 610 + 705 = _____

7. Richard went shopping and spent £12.60 on food, £5.50 on some socks and £10 on a scarf.
How much money did he have left out of £30?

   £ _____

8. Calculate the answer to the multiplication below.

$$
\begin{array}{r}
4731 \\
\times \quad 19 \\
\hline
\end{array}
$$

9. Work out the answer to the division below.

$$21\,|\overline{1428}$$

10. Andy puts £500 in a bank account. The money earns 8% interest per year.
How much money does Andy have in the account after one year's interest is added?

£ _____

/10

Mixed 2

1. Order these decimals, starting with the **smallest**.

   a)   3.2   3.11   3.67   3.09   3.049

   b)   80.7   80.81   84.38   80.06   84.5

2. Estimate how much water is in this jug.

   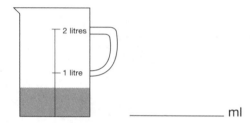

   _____ ml

3. $3b = 4a + c + 12$

   Find the value of b when $a = 7$ and $c = 2$.

   $b =$ _____

4. Write in the missing fraction.

   $\frac{1}{5} + \frac{1}{3} +$ ☐ $= 1$

5. Convert the following quantities into decimal form.

   a)   7180 g   _____ kg

   b)   254 g   _____ kg

   c)   5888 ml   _____ litres

   d)   3469 cm   _____ m

6. Amy goes to the cinema and spends £5.40 on watching a film. She also buys a bag of sweets which costs £1.85.

   How much does Amy spend altogether?

   £ _____

Mixed 2

7. Take away 844 273 from 1 105 312.

8. Calculate the answer to the following multiplication.

```
    1914
x     35
```

9. Work out the answer to the division below.

```
42 | 4788
```

10. A rope is 120 m long. The length is increased by 50% when another rope is tied to it. How long is the rope now?

_____ m

/10

Crossword fun

Try this maths crossword, using the clues below.

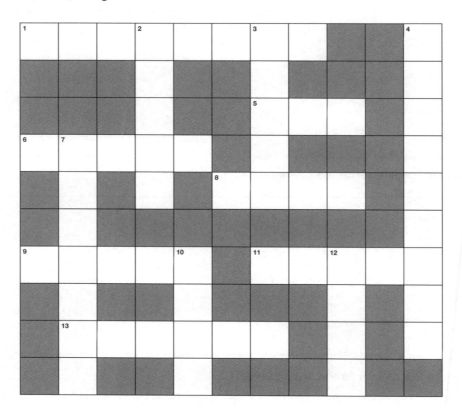

Across

1. Any three-sided polygon. (8)
5. The product of 5 and 2. (3)
6. $104 - 8^2$ (5)
8. Nothing at all. (4)
9. A square-based pyramid has five of these. (5)
11. Add all the numbers in a sum together to get this. (5)
13. The point of intersection of the x and y axis. (6)

Down

2. An angle of less than 90°. (5)
3. The metric version of a pint. (5)
4. Any polygon with sides of different lengths has this property. (9)
7. Any shape with eight sides. (7)
10. Another name for an operation in a calculation. (4)
12. The units for this could be seconds. (4)

Wordsearch fun

Can you find all the maths terms in this wordsearch?

D	E	I	M	P	R	O	P	E	R	F	R	A	C	T	I	O	N	B	E
D	E	G	A	F	S	R	R	Y	L	F	S	T	N	I	O	P	S	E	E
I	P	G	L	A	W	I	E	Q	U	A	L	V	B	C	F	A	D	O	T
V	L	Q	R	C	A	G	G	S	A	W	W	G	A	R	L	I	N	G	U
I	Q	F	B	E	S	I	E	Z	M	U	S	D	E	D	O	M	N	E	N
S	O	K	O	V	E	N	T	T	Q	R	M	Q	F	B	D	H	N	O	I
I	I	I	Z	D	V	C	N	A	O	R	E	P	U	A	R	P	O	M	M
O	Y	T	G	L	E	P	I	L	I	N	D	C	F	D	D	A	G	E	C
N	A	E	M	J	N	Y	I	L	C	O	I	P	A	R	O	R	Y	T	H
A	L	A	F	J	R	W	U	Y	U	I	A	T	D	I	E	G	L	R	L
K	I	L	O	M	E	T	R	E	C	X	N	R	Q	H	E	R	O	Y	W
C	T	A	C	T	Y	N	C	K	K	V	O	R	H	T	N	A	P	P	O
E	R	C	O	O	R	A	T	I	O	N	A	A	F	J	S	B	N	F	J
R	E	W	O	D	F	T	S	S	N	I	C	L	O	C	K	W	I	S	E
E	A	F	J	M	B	S	P	O	D	U	E	U	F	S	O	I	A	V	L
T	Z	X	V	I	P	P	G	S	T	N	Q	G	A	O	R	D	D	Z	C
R	L	A	A	H	L	A	I	A	G	P	U	E	S	R	A	T	I	A	R
A	P	E	E	I	N	W	S	T	I	N	U	R	D	E	Z	H	N	L	I
U	A	R	Y	O	D	R	H	S	F	F	S	D	W	Z	T	S	P	W	C
Q	E	A	N	E	G	A	T	I	V	E	T	A	I	H	E	I	G	H	T

Area	Geometry	Origin
Bar graph	Height	Polygon
Compass	Improper fraction	Point
Circle	Integer	Quarter
Clockwise	Kilometre	Ratio
Cuboid	Kite	Regular
Division	Litre	Sphere
Degree	Length	Sum
Edge	Median	Tally
Equal	Minute	Third
Even	Negative	Unit
Face	Nonagon	Width
		Zero

1. Fill in the gaps to make the following sentences correct.

   A three-sided polygon is a _____ .

   An eight-sided polygon is an _____ .

   A five-sided polygon is a _____ .

   A seven-sided polygon is a _____ .

   A ten-sided polygon is a _____ .

2. An equilateral triangle has a perimeter of 45 cm. What is the length of each side?

   _____ cm

3. Look at the following shapes and match each of them to the correct description.

          has no lines of symmetry

          not a polygon

          interior angles add to make 180°

          is a quadrilateral

          is a pentagon

4. On the grid below, complete the drawing to make an irregular quadrilateral.

   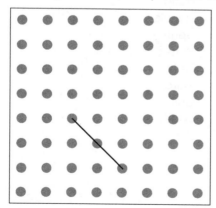

5. The radius of a circle is 54 cm. What is the diameter of the circle?

Diameter = _____

6. Put a tick in the shapes which have any parallel sides.

7. Here are five shapes. Tick the two which have lines of symmetry.

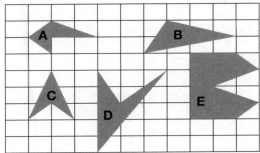

8. How many squares that each have a perimeter of 26 cm will fit into the rectangle below?

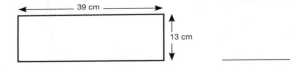

_____

9. Look at this circle inside a square. What is the radius of the circle if the square has a perimeter of 32 cm?

Radius = _____ cm

10. Angle $c = 90°$ and angle $b = 60°$, so what is angle a?

$a =$ _____°

/10

3-D shapes

1. How many **faces** do the following 3-D shapes have?

   a) Cube _____ face(s)

   b) Cylinder _____ face(s)

   c) Sphere _____ face(s)

2. How many **edges** do the following 3-D shapes have?

   a) Cuboid _____ edge(s)

   b) Cone _____ edge(s)

   c) Square-based pyramid _____ edge(s)

3. How many **vertices** do the following 3-D shapes have?

   a) Cylinder _____ vertices

   b) Cube _____ vertices

   c) Triangular-based pyramid _____ vertices

4. Which two of the following are correct nets for a cube?

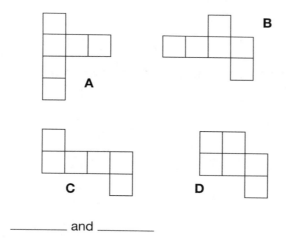

B

A

C

D

_____ and _____

5. What is the volume of a cube with an edge that measures 7 cm?

   _____ cm^3

6. What is the surface area of this cuboid?

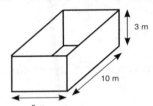

9 cm

8 cm

5 cm

_____ cm²

7. What is the volume of this open-top tank?

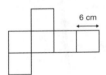

3 m

10 m

5 m

_____ m³

8. A cube has a volume of 1000 cm³. What is the area of each face?

_____ cm²

9. What is the volume of the cube which has this net?

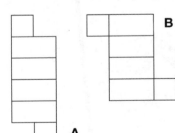

6 cm

_____ cm³

10. Which of the following are correct nets for a cuboid?

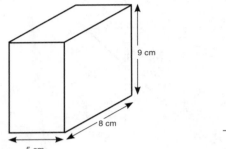

B

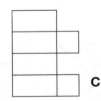

D

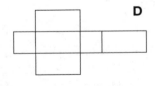

C

A

_____ and _____

/10

1. Using a ruler, complete the diagram below to make a symmetrical shape.

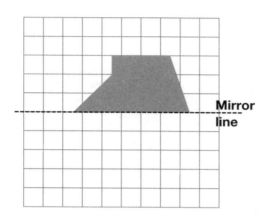

Mirror line

2. Using a ruler, draw the reflection of this shape.

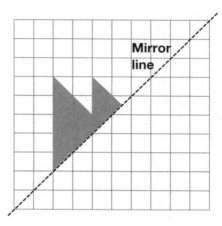

Mirror line

3. Look at the shapes below and put a tick inside the shapes with at least one line of symmetry.

4. Which of these letters are symmetrical?

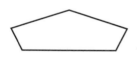  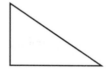

F H B J _____ and _____

5. Look at the shape in the diagram below left. Write the letter of the shape that would be its reflection.

Letter _____

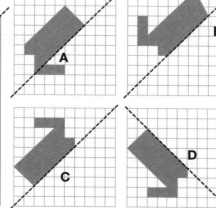

Mirror line

Geometry and angles 1

6. Join the angles to the correct labels.

reflex angle
acute angle
right angle
obtuse angle

7. Estimate the size of the acute angles below. Do not use a protractor.

$x =$ _____ °

$y =$ _____ °

8. Estimate the size of the obtuse angles below. Do not use a protractor.

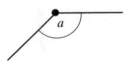

$a =$ _____ °

$b =$ _____ °

9. Look at the parallelogram below and calculate the angle x. Do not use a protractor.

$x =$ _____ °

70°

x

10. Calculate angle x in this isosceles triangle.
Do not use a protractor.

$x =$ _____ °

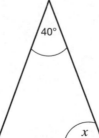

40°

x

/10

Geometry and angles 2

1. Measure angle x accurately. Use a protractor.

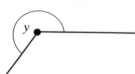

$x =$ _____ °

2. Measure angle z accurately. Use a protractor.

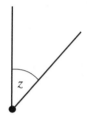

$z =$ _____ °

3. Measure all the angles in this triangle. Use a protractor.

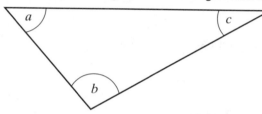

$a =$ _____ °

$b =$ _____ °

$c =$ _____ °

4. Measure angle y accurately. Use a protractor.

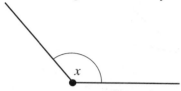

$y =$ _____ °

5. Measure accurately the two angles below. Use a protractor.

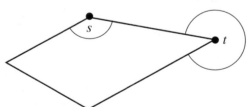

$s =$ _____ °

$t =$ _____ °

6. Calculate the angle x in the triangle below.

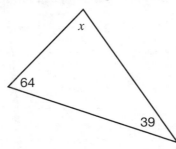

$x =$ _____ °

7. Look at the following regular polygon. What is the internal angle z?

$z =$ _____ °

8. Calculate the angle x in the pentagon below.

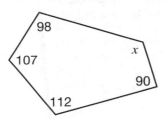

$x =$ _____ °

9. Calculate the angle t.

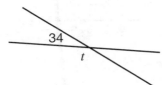

$t =$ _____ °

10. Calculate the angle z.

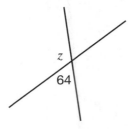

$z =$ _____ °

/10

Coordinates

1. Plot these coordinates on the grid below.

J (1 , 7)   K (6 , 5)
L (9 , 13)   M (4 , 10)

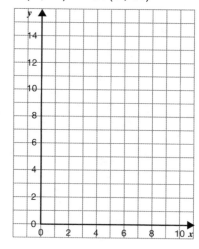

2.

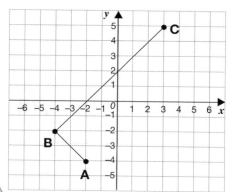

a) Where is the park? (,   )

b) Where is the market? (,   )

c) Where is the pool? (,   )

3. Write down the coordinates M, N, O and P.

M = (,   )   N = (,   )
O = (,   )   P = (,   )

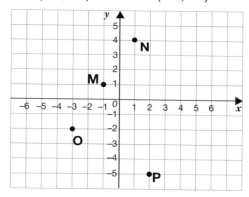

4. Plot point M on the grid below to complete the square JKLM.

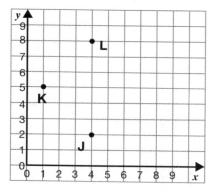

5. Plot point D on the grid below and complete the rectangle ABCD.

Coordinates

6. Which quadrants are the letters A, B, C and D in?

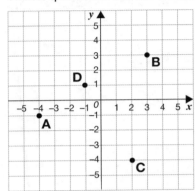

A = Quadrant _____

B = Quadrant _____

C = Quadrant _____

D = Quadrant _____

7. Draw the triangle below reflected in the x axis.

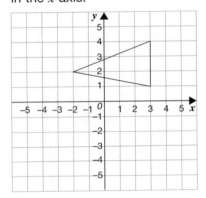

8. Plot the points A, B, C and D on the graph below.

A (4 , −3)   B (−1 , 2)
C (−4 , −1)   D (1 , 2)

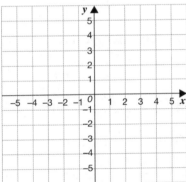

9. Plot the points A, B, C, D, E, and F then join them together to make the capital letter E.

A (2 , 2)   B (−2 , 2)
C (−2 , −1)   D (2 , −1)
E (−2 , −4)   F (2 , −4)

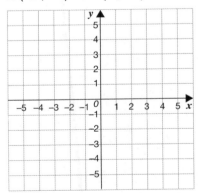

10. Translate the shape below so that Point A is at (1 , 2).

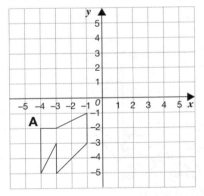

/10

Reading scales and converting units

1. Convert these units of length.

   a) 3 m = _____ cm

   b) 45 mm = _____ cm

   c) 3.5 km = _____ m

   d) 4 miles = _____ km

2. Convert these units of weight.

   a) 3500 g = _____ kg

   b) 750 kg = _____ tonnes

   c) 4.06 kg = _____ g

   d) 4.2 tonnes = _____ kg

3. Convert these units of capacity.

   a) 3.5 cl = _____ ml

   b) 3450 ml = _____ litres

   c) 9.052 litres = _____ ml

   d) 457 ml = _____ cl

4. What is the reading on the scale below?

   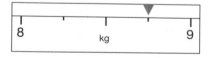

   _____ kg

5. How much water is in this jug?

   _____ litres

Reading scales and converting units

6. Measure the lengths of these three lines with a ruler.

a) _____   _____

b) _____   _____

c) _____   _____

7. How much more flour do you need to add to these kitchen scales to make 1.9 kg?

_____

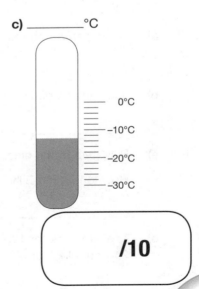

8. When opened, a tap lets 100 ml of water through every second. How much water passes through the open tap in 2.5 minutes? _____ ml

9. A man walks 1.4 km to work every day and at the end of the day walks back home again. How many kilometres does the man walk in a normal five-day working week?

_____ km

How many miles is this equivalent to? _____ miles

10. Write down the readings on these three thermometers.

a) _____°C   b) _____°C   c) _____°C

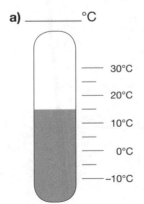
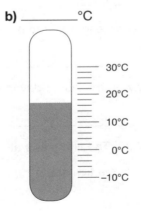

/10

1. What fraction of 3 hours is 30 minutes?

   $$\frac{\Box}{\Box}$$

2. How many seconds are there in 45 minutes?

   _____ seconds

3. Jon sets off from school at 3:30 p.m. He then goes to see his Grandma and eventually gets home at 19:45.

   How many minutes after Jon left school did he arrive at home?

   _____ minutes

4. How many minutes are there in 24 hours?

   _____ minutes

5. Here is a calendar for the month of September in a particular year.

September						
Sun	Mon	Tue	Wed	Thu	Fri	Sat
			1	2	3	4
5	6	7	8	9	10	11
12	13	14	15	16	17	18
19	20	21	22	23	24	25
26	27	28	29	30		

   a) School starts on the second Wednesday of the month. What date is that?

   _____

   b) Jack arrives back from holiday on the last Friday in August. What date is that?

   _____

6. a) Billy gets to the cinema at 17:30. The film starts at 18:25.

   How long must Billy wait before the film starts?

   _____ minutes

   b) The film lasts for 115 minutes. What time does it finish? Give your answer in 24-hour clock time.

   _____

7. Here is a calendar for the month of July in a particular year.

July						
Sun	Mon	Tue	Wed	Thu	Fri	Sat
				1	2	3
4	5	6	7	8	9	10
11	12	13	14	15	16	17
18	19	20	21	22	23	24
25	26	27	28	29	30	31

Sally goes on holiday for 10 days, and she arrives back on the 4th of July.
What day of the week did Sally leave on?

_____

8. What is $\frac{2}{3}$ of 2 hours? _____

9. Sasha can run a kilometre in 4 minutes and 15 seconds.
If Sasha always runs at the same speed, how long will it take her to run 7 kilometres?

_____

10. James puts on a DVD at twenty-five past five. The DVD finishes at quarter to eight.
How many minutes does the DVD last for?

_____ minutes

/10

Perimeter, area and volume

1. What is the perimeter of the shape below?

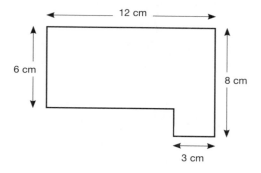

_____ cm

2. Look at this shape on the centimetre square grid.

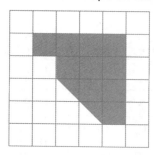

What is the area of this shape?

_____ cm²

3. A regular pentagon has a perimeter of 32 cm.

What is the length of each side of the pentagon? _____ cm

4. Estimate the area of the shape below.

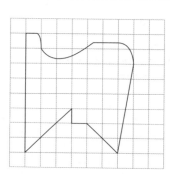

Area = _____ squares

5. Look at this shape on a centimetre square grid.

What is the perimeter of this shape?

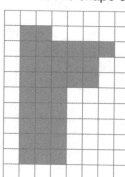

_____ cm

Perimeter, area and volume

6. Look at the cube below and calculate its volume and surface area.

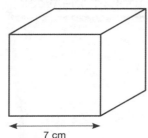

Volume = _____ cm³

Area = _____ cm²

7 cm

7. Tick the two shapes below which have the same area.

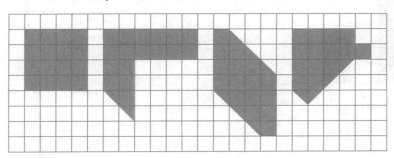

8. Tick the two shapes below which have the same perimeter.

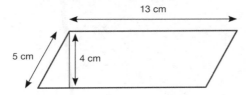

9. Calculate the area of this parallelogram.

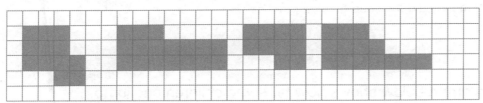

13 cm

5 cm

4 cm

Area = _____ cm²

10. What is the area of the isosceles triangle here? _____ cm²

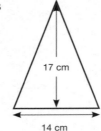

17 cm

14 cm

/10

Tables, charts and graphs 1

> The bar graph below shows the amount of money a shop took in one week.

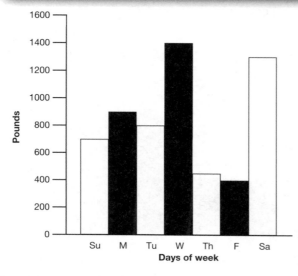

1. How much money did the shop take at the weekend?

   £ _____

2. How much money did the shop take on Monday?

   £ _____

> The bar line graph below shows how far some children can jump.

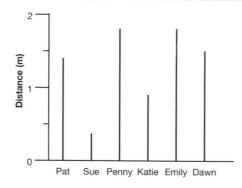

3. How far can Emily jump? _____ m

4. How much further can Pat jump than Katie? _____ m

Tables, charts and graphs 1

The line graph shows the accumulative rainfall during March in one year.

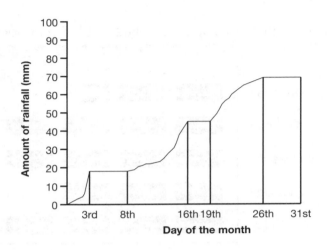

5. How much rainfall was there in the whole month? _____ mm

6. How much rainfall was there between the 16th and 31st of the month? _____ mm

7. Why does the graph flatten off in three places?

   _____

8. True or false? There were 21 wet days during the month. _____

There are 300 ice lollipops of four different types in a freezer. The number of each type is represented by the chart.

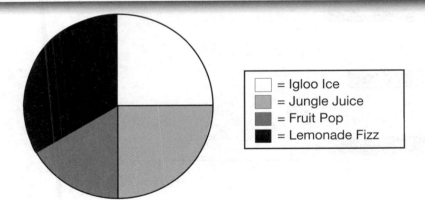

= Igloo Ice
= Jungle Juice
= Fruit Pop
= Lemonade Fizz

9. How many Jungle Juice lollipops are there? _____

10. Approximately how many Fruit Pop lollipops are there? _____

/10

Tables, charts and graphs 2

The number of chocolate bars sold at a school tuck shop is shown below.

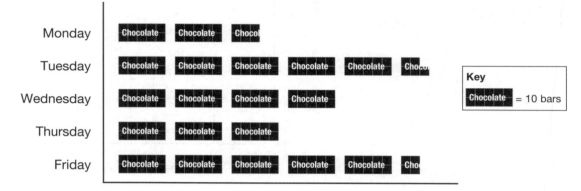

1. How many chocolate bars were sold on Monday?

_____ bars

2. How many more chocolate bars were sold on Friday than on Wednesday?

_____ bars

Look at the bar chart showing pocket money received by six children.

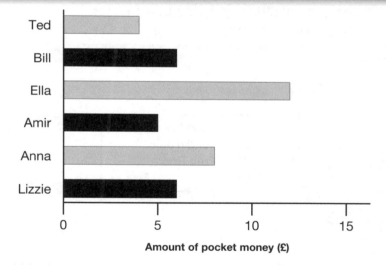

Amount of pocket money (£)

3. How much pocket money did Bill get?   £ _____

4. How much money did the children receive altogether?   £ _____

Tables, charts and graphs 2

The pie chart below shows the type of pets 100 children have.

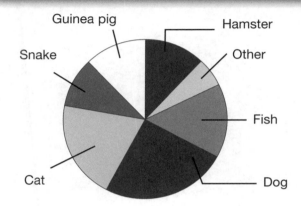

5. Approximately how many children have a dog or a cat?   _____

6. Estimate the number of children who have a pet snake.   _____

7. Estimate how many more children have a dog than a hamster.   _____

The temperature in a conservatory was measured regularly and recorded on the graph.

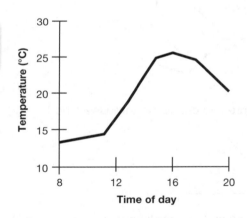

8. At what time was the last temperature reading taken?   _____

9. What was the approximate temperature at 4 p.m.?   _____°C

10. When did the temperature first reach 20°C?   _____

/10

Mixed 3

1. Draw all the diagonals on the octagon below.

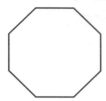

2. What is the volume of this cuboid?

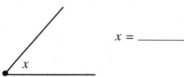

Volume = _____ cm³

3. Use a ruler and draw the reflection of this shape.

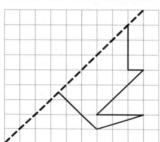

4. Measure angle x accurately. Use a protractor.

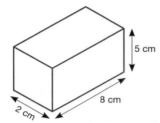

$x =$ _____ °

5. Write down the coordinates of A, B, C and D.

A = (,   )   B = (,   )   C = (,   )   D = (,   )

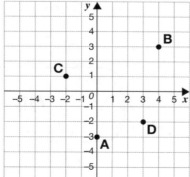

Mixed 3

6. Calculate the mean in this list of 10 numbers.

   8, 7, 7, 9, 4, 12, 10, 7, 11, 9 _____

7. Measure the lengths of these three lines with a ruler.

   a)  _____ cm

   b) _____ cm

   c) _____ cm

8. What fraction of 2 hours is 15 minutes?

9. A group of children do a sponsored walk. Here is the amount of money each child raised:

Name	Amount (£)
Jess	10.20
Kate	12.90
Paul	8.50
Wendy	14.00
Raul	13.40

   What is the mean amount of money raised per child? £_____

10. What is the area of this right-angled triangle?

    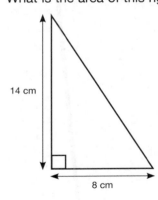

    14 cm

    8 cm

    Area = _____ cm²

    /10

Mixed 4

1. Angle $a = 40°$ and angle $b = 141°$. What is angle c?

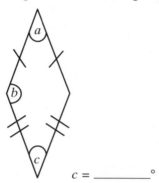

    $c =$ _____ °

2. What is the volume of a cube with this net?

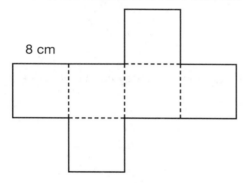

    8 cm

    Volume = _____ cm³

3. Estimate the size of the angles below. Do not use a protractor.

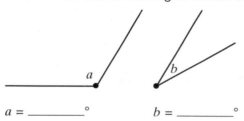

    $a =$ _____ ° $b =$ _____ °

4. Calculate the angle x in the triangle below.

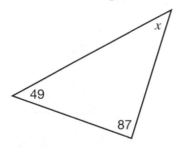

    49

    87

    $x =$ _____ °

Mixed 4

5. Plot the points D, E, F and G on the graph below.

D (–2 , –4)   E (3 , –2)   F (0 , 3)   G (–2 , 2)

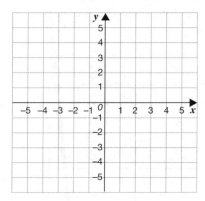

6. Find the mean of this set of 10 numbers.

15, 12, 8, 15, 8, 10, 10, 17, 13, 20 _____

7. What is the reading on the scale below?

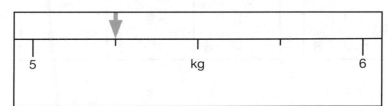

_____ kg

8. Micky sets off for work at 7:30 a.m. He arrives at work at 8:55 a.m. How many minutes after Micky left home did he arrive at work?

_____ minutes

9. Find the mean of this set of numbers.

3, 8, 4, 3, 2, 4, 7, 6, 9, 5, 4 _____

10. Calculate the area of this parallelogram.

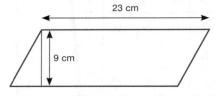

Area = _____ cm²

/10

Sudoku fun

Each of these puzzles will take about 10 minutes!

Sudoku is a logic puzzle. It is presented as a square grid with 9 squares to a side. Thick grid lines emphasise each block of 9 squares. The grid is partially filled with the numbers 1 through to 9. To solve the puzzle, the empty squares are filled in so that each row, column and block contains each of the numbers 1 through to 9. There is only one correct answer.

29.

	8			2	7		3	1
		7	9	1	4		6	
1				3	8			5
7	6	8	2	4	1		9	3
			3	5	6	7		
4	3	5	8		9	2	1	6
6		3	4		2	1		
	7	2	1		5		4	
5							2	8

30.

5		2	7			9	3	
1				2			7	
	7	9		3	1	6	8	2
6	8	5	1			7	2	
			9		7			
	9	3			2	1	4	6
9	2	1	3	7		4	6	
	5			9				3
	4	6			5	8		7

31.

9		6	1	4	8		3	
			2				6	1
	8	2	3	6		4		
4	2		5	7		1		3
8				3				5
3		5		8	2		7	4
			5	4	3	2		
2	7			9				
	3		6	2	1	9		7

32.

3		5		8	7		1	
2		6				4	7	
	1		2	4			8	6
8		2		9		3		
	6	4	3		2	8	9	
		3		6		7		2
4	3	1		5	9		2	
	2	8				9		7
	9		8	2	6			4

Fun with squares

How many squares can you find on the picture below? Look carefully, there are more than you think!

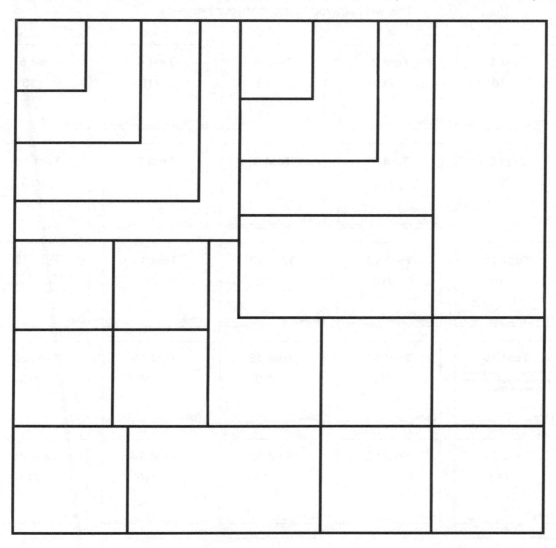

_____ squares

Progress report

Record how many questions you got right and the date you completed each test.
This will help you to monitor your progress.

Test 1 /10 Date _____	**Test 2** /10 Date _____	**Test 3** /10 Date _____	**Test 4** /10 Date _____	**Test 5** /10 Date _____
Test 6 /10 Date _____	**Test 7** /10 Date _____	**Test 8** /10 Date _____	**Test 9** /10 Date _____	**Test 10** /10 Date _____
Test 11 /10 Date _____	**Test 12** /10 Date _____	**Test 13** /10 Date _____	**Test 14** /10 Date _____	**Test 15** If you got all of the clues in less than 10 minutes, score yourself 10 marks. Date _____
Test 16 If you got all of the clues in less than 10 minutes, score yourself 10 marks. Date _____	**Test 17** /10 Date _____	**Test 18** /10 Date _____	**Test 19** /10 Date _____	**Test 20** /10 Date _____
Test 21 /10 Date _____	**Test 22** /10 Date _____	**Test 23** /10 Date _____	**Test 24** /10 Date _____	**Test 25** /10 Date _____
Test 26 /10 Date _____	**Test 27** /10 Date _____	**Test 28** /10 Date _____	**Test 29** If you complete the puzzle in less than 10 minutes, score yourself 10 marks. Date _____	**Test 30** If you complete the puzzle in less than 10 minutes, score yourself 10 marks. Date _____
Test 31 If you complete the puzzle in less than 10 minutes, score yourself 10 marks. Date _____	**Test 32** If you complete the puzzle in less than 10 minutes, score yourself 10 marks. Date _____	**Test 33** If you found the right number of squares in less than 10 minutes, score yourself 10 marks. Date _____		

Answers: Maths 10-Minute Tests, age 10-11

Test 1
1. 10 835
2. **a)** two hundred **b)** two thousand **c)** twenty thousand
3. **a)** 1553 **b)** 4224 **c)** 3530
4. **a)** 1067, 2799, 2809, 2851, 4001
   b) 6001, 6099, 6430, 6515, 7000
5. **a)** 1 031 710, 103 826, 87 271, 17 001, 12 483
   b) 4 280 338, 2 984 988, 583 200, 560 200, 100 999
6. **a)** 4.03, 4.09, 4.099, 4.2, 4.27
   b) 20.01, 20.72, 20.9, 24.27, 24.4
7. $\frac{7}{2}$, $\frac{12}{5}$, $\frac{7}{3}$, $\frac{3}{2}$, $\frac{10}{9}$
8. **a)** Billy **b)** Eric **c)** Jon
9. **a)** B **b)** A **c)** D
10. **a)** Grant **b)** Smith

Test 2
1. **a)** 440, 370, 900, 250
   b) 6480, 7050, 8890, 5810
   c) 29 840, 18 000, 21 000, 99 510
2. **a)** 200, 1000, 700, 300
   b) 5800, 4200, 6700, 3400
   c) 23 100, 57 900, 31 000, 90 000
   d) 128 300, 451 200, 927 000, 370 000
3. **a)** 1000, 3000, 6000, 8000
   b) 12 000, 30 000, 68 000, 37 000
   c) 222 000, 709 000, 502 000, 199 000
4. Child 1 = 1.2 m, Child 2 = 1.3 m, Child 3 = 1.2 m
   Child 4 = 1.4 m, Child 5 = 1.3 m, Child 6 = 1.5 m
5.

Question	Estimate (between these numbers)	Answer
2129 + 3454	5300 to 5700	5583
24 783 + 15 031	39 000 to 40 000	39 814
7.92 + 15.01	22 to 23	22.93
5203 − 3487	1500 to 2000	1716

6. Answers between 2100 ml and 2400 ml
7. Answers between 12 kg and 14 kg
8. Answers between 180 cm and 190 cm
9. Answers between 60 minutes and 62.5 minutes
10. Answers between 2500 weeks and 2600 weeks

Test 3
1.

3	6	12	24	**48**	**96**

2.

160	80	40	20	**10**	**5**

3.

□	○	△	□	○	△	□

4.

−14	−8	**−2**	4	10	16

Test 4
1. 67
2. 216
3. 40
4. Blue marbles = 25
   Yellow marbles = 75
5. Adults = 50   Children = 150
6. **a)** 4, 8, 12, 16, 20, 24, 28, 32, 36
   b) 28 and 1, 14 and 2, 7 and 4
7. Shortest = 9 cm   Longest = 18 cm
8. 4 years old
9. 18
10. 42

Test 5
1. 8.2
2. **a)** five hundredths
   b) five tenths
   c) five thousandths
3. **a)** 0.6 **b)** 2.8 **c)** 7.64 **d)** 0.18
4. **a)** 3.6 **b)** 20.4 **c)** 42.7 **d)** 26.04
5. **a)** 1.6 **b)** 11.2 **c)** 13.89 **d)** 37.83
6.

	Old amount	New amount
Carrots	1200 g	2.4 kg
Potatoes	2.5 kg	5 kg
Tomatoes	0.45 kg	0.9 kg
Onions	3	6
Peas	300 g	0.6 kg

7. £71.56
8. 163.63 kg
9. 220 litres
10. 170 m

Test 6
1. **a)** 71 **b)** 109 **c)** 143
2. **a)** 436 **b)** 729 **c)** 1235
3. **a)** 106 **b)** 122 **c)** 101
4. **a)** 10 352 **b)** 47 101 **c)** 107 891
5. 251 815
6. £7.35
7. £79.39
8. 155 m
9. £17.02
10. 829 + 164 = 993

Test 7
1. **a)** 46 **b)** 58 **c)** 33
2. **a)** 213 **b)** 239 **c)** 146
3. **a)** 48 **b)** 16 **c)** 42
4. **a)** 715 **b)** 68 556 **c)** 607 569
5. 797 788
6. £7.73
7. £3.60

Test 3 (continued)
5.

13	5	**−3**	−11	−19	**−27**

6. 8°C
7. 8°C
8. −5°C
9. 6°C
10. 24 hours

8. 3.3 kg
9. 8 minutes
10. 944 − 398 = 546

Test 8
1. $4\frac{2}{7}$
2. $\frac{5}{8}$
3. $1\frac{5}{12}$
4. $3\frac{7}{10}$
5. $\frac{1}{2}$
6. **a)** $\frac{1}{6}$ **b)** $\frac{1}{8}$ **c)** $\frac{1}{16}$
7. $\frac{3}{2}$ $\frac{13}{6}$ $\frac{29}{8}$ $\frac{19}{5}$ $\frac{12}{3}$
8. $\frac{4}{15}$ or $\frac{8}{30}$
9. $\frac{7}{24}$
10. $3\frac{1}{2}$ or $3\frac{6}{12}$ or $\frac{42}{12}$

Test 9
1. **a)** 27.1, 271, 2710 **b)** 30.9, 309, 3090 **c)** 460, 4600, 46000
2. 40 066
3. 105 915
4. 361 974
5. £20 784
6. £601.64
7. 45 kg or 45 000 g
8. £282.91
9. 16.383 l or 16 383 ml
10. 28.635 m

Test 10
1. **a)** 2.4, 0.24, 0.024 **b)** 35.7, 3.57, 0.357 **c)** 259.8, 25.98, 2.598
2. 82
3. 37
4. 83
5. 148
6. £27
7. 0.125 kg or 125 g
8. £27
9. 16 litres
10. 61

Test 11
1. **a)** 50% **b)** 25% **c)** 30% **d)** 75%
2. **a)** 34% **b)** 57% **c)** 70% **d)** 3%
3. **a)** 0.49 **b)** 0.72 **c)** 0.05 **d)** 0.6
4. **a)** 10% **b)** 32% **c)** 23% **d)** 65%
5. **a)** 21 kg **b)** 32 litres **c)** 1.5 km **d)** £35
6. **a)** £36 **b)** 60 m **c)** £1.20 **d)** 180 kg
7. £2
8. £321
9. 82.8 kg
10. 1000 km

Test 12
1. $\frac{6}{16}$ or $\frac{3}{8}$
2. $\frac{5}{8}$
3. 6:4 or 3:2
4. 24
5. 24:16 or 12:8 or 6:4 or 3:2
6. 10:6 or 5:3
7. $\frac{6}{16}$ or $\frac{3}{8}$

8. Boys = 9, Girls = 9
9. 6
10. 7:5

Test 13
1. a) one thousand b) five hundred thousand c) eight million
2.

Question	Estimate	Answer
6138 + 8432	14 500	14 570
36 867 + 13 014	50 000	49 881
4.97 + 18.01	23	22.98
8211 − 7501	700	710

3. 69
4. $\frac{1}{2}$
5. 183.39 kg
6. a) 673 b) 958 c) 1315
7. £1.90
8. 89 889
9. 68
10. £540

Test 14
1. a) 3.049, 3.09, 3.11, 3.2, 3.67
   b) 80.06, 80.7, 80.81, 84.38, 84.5
2. Answers between 600 ml and 720 ml
3. 14
4. $\frac{7}{15}$
5. a) 7.18 kg b) 0.254 kg c) 5.888 litres d) 34.69 m
6. £7.25
7. 261 039
8. 66 990
9. 114
10. 180 m

Test 15

T	R	I	A	N	G	L	E			I
		C				I				R
		U				T	E	N		R
F	O	R	T	Y		R				E
	C		E		Z	E	R	O		G
	T									U
F	A	C	E	S		T	O	T	A	L
	G			I				I		A
	O	R	I	G	I	N		M		R
	N			N				E		

Test 16

```
D   I M P R O P E R F R A C T I O N
D E     F   R R         T N I O P       E
I   G   A   I E Q U A L         D   T
V     R C   G G             I     G U
I     E   I E   M U S       O     E N
S K     E N T T     M     B   H N O I
I I   D V   N A     E   U     P O M M
O   T G   E   I L       D C   D A G E
N   E     N       L       I   R R Y T
L               Y       A     I G L R
K I L O M E T R E       N     H R O Y
T                   R   T   A P
R C     R A T I O     A       B
R E   O         N   C L O C K W I S E
E     M   S O     E U         I     L
T     P   G   N   G O       D     C
R A   H A   G     E   R T       R
A E E N   S T I N U R   E H       I
U R O     H S         Z         C
Q E A N E G A T I V E       H E I G H T
```

Test 17
1. A three-sided polygon is a *triangle*. An eight-sided polygon is an *octagon*. A five-sided polygon is a *pentagon*. A seven-sided polygon is a *heptagon*. A ten-sided polygon is a *decagon*.
2. 15 cm
3.

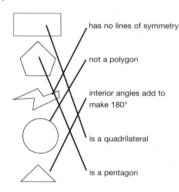

   has no lines of symmetry
   not a polygon
   interior angles add to make 180°
   is a quadrilateral
   is a pentagon

4. Any four-sided shape with at least one side a different length.
5. 108 cm or 1.08 m
6.

7.

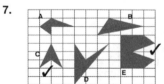

8. 12
9. 4 cm
10. 105°

Test 18
1. a) 6 b) 3 c) 1
2. a) 12 b) 1 c) 8
3. a) 0 b) 8 c) 4
4. B and C
5. 343 cm³
6. 314 cm²
7. 150 m³
8. 100 cm²
9. 216 cm³
10. B and D

Test 19
1.

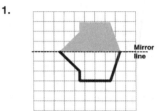

2.

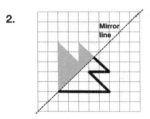

3.

4. H and B
5. C
6.

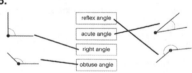

   reflex angle
   acute angle
   right angle
   obtuse angle

7. Answers in between the following: $x = 20°$ to $30°$ and $y = 65°$ to $75°$
8. Answers in between the following: $a = 130°$ to $140°$ and $b = 95°$ to $105°$
9. 110°
10. 70°

Test 20
1. 130° (126° to 134° is acceptable)
2. 40° (36° to 44° is acceptable)
3. $a = 50°$ $b = 100°$ $c = 30°$
   (Answers ± 3°)
4. 235° (Answers ± 4°)
5. $s = 140°$ $t = 320°$
   (Answers ± 4°)
6. 77°
7. 120°
8. 133°
9. 146°
10. 116°

Test 21
1.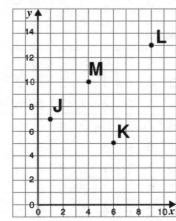
2. a) Park (17, 12) b) Market (3, 13)
   c) Pool (16, 1)
3. M = (–1, 1) N = (1, 4) O = (–3, –2)
   P = (2, –5)
4.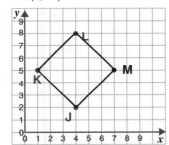
5.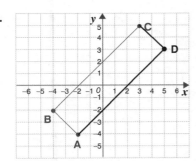
6. A = III, B = I, C = IV, D = II

7.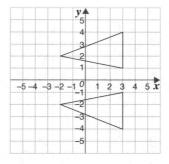

8.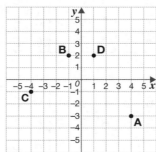

9.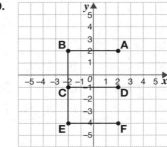

10.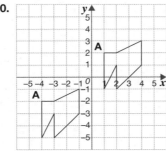

Test 22
1. a) 300 cm b) 4.5 cm c) 3500 m
   d) 6.45 km
2. a) 3.5 kg b) 0.75 tonnes c) 4060 g
   d) 4200 kg
3. a) 35 ml b) 3.45 litres c) 9052 ml
   d) 45.7 cl
4. 8.75 kg or 8 kg 750 g
5. 2.2 litres or 2 litres and 200 ml
6. a) 7.6 cm or 76 mm b) 4.2 cm or
   42 mm c) 5.5 cm or 55 mm
7. 1.1 kg or 1 kg 100 g or 1100 g
8. 15 000 ml
9. 14 km, 8.68 miles
10. a) 15°C b) 17°C c) –13°C

Test 23
1. $\frac{1}{6}$
2. 2700 seconds
3. 255 minutes
4. 1440 minutes
5. a) 8th September
   b) 27th August
6. a) 55 minutes
   b) 20:20
7. Thursday
8. 80 minutes or 1 hour and 20
   minutes
9. 29 minutes and 45 seconds
10. 140 minutes

Test 24
1. 40 cm
2. 11 cm²
3. 6.4 cm
4. 35-39 squares
5. 30 cm
6. Volume 343 cm³, Area 294 cm²
7.
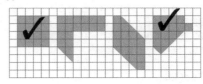
8.
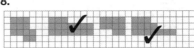
9. 52 cm²
10. 119 cm²

Test 25
1. £2000
2. £900
3. 1.8 m
4. 0.5 m
5. 69 mm (accept 68 to 70)
6. 24 mm (accept 22 to 27)
7. It did not rain on those days.
8. false
9. 75
10. 50 (accept 45 to 55)

Test 26
1. 26
2. 14
3. £6
4. £41 (accept 40 to 42)
5. 45 (accept 42 to 48)
6. 10 (accept 7 to 13)
7. 13 (accept 10 to 15)
8. 20:00 or 8 p.m.
9. 26°C (accept 25°C to 27°C)
10. Answers between 12:45 and 13:45
    (12:45 p.m. and 1:45 p.m.)

Test 27

1.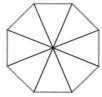

2. 80 cm³

3.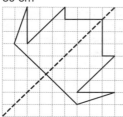

4. 50°
5. A = (0 , –3) B = (4, 3) C = (–2, 1)
   D = (3, –2)
6. 8.4
7. **a)** 4.3 cm **b)** 2.8 cm **c)** 5.1 cm
8. $\frac{1}{8}$
9. £11.80
10. 56 cm²

Test 28

1. 38°
2. 512 cm³
3. Accept a = 115°–125°, and b = 25°–35°
4. 44°
5.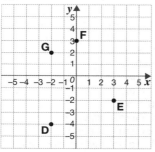

6. 12.8
7. 5.25 kg
8. 85 minutes
9. 5
10. 207 cm²

Test 29

9	8	6	5	2	7	4	3	1
3	5	7	9	1	4	8	6	2
1	2	4	6	3	8	9	7	5
7	6	8	2	4	1	5	9	3
2	1	9	3	5	6	7	8	4
4	3	5	8	7	9	2	1	6
6	9	3	4	8	2	1	5	7
8	7	2	1	6	5	3	4	9
5	4	1	7	9	3	6	2	8

Test 30

5	6	2	7	8	4	9	3	1
1	3	8	6	2	9	5	7	4
4	7	9	5	3	1	6	8	2
6	8	5	1	4	3	7	2	9
2	1	4	9	6	7	3	5	8
7	9	3	8	5	2	1	4	6
9	2	1	3	7	8	4	6	5
8	5	7	4	9	6	2	1	3
3	4	6	2	1	5	8	9	7

Test 31

9	5	6	1	4	8	7	3	2
7	4	3	2	9	5	8	6	1
1	8	2	3	6	7	4	5	9
4	2	9	5	7	6	1	8	3
8	6	7	4	1	3	2	9	5
3	1	5	9	8	2	6	7	4
6	9	1	7	5	4	3	2	8
2	7	4	8	3	9	5	1	6
5	3	8	6	2	1	9	4	7

Test 32

3	4	5	6	8	7	2	1	9
2	8	6	9	1	5	4	7	3
7	1	9	2	4	3	5	8	6
8	7	2	5	9	4	3	6	1
1	6	4	3	7	2	8	9	5
9	5	3	1	6	8	7	4	2
4	3	1	7	5	9	6	2	8
6	2	8	4	3	1	9	5	7
5	9	7	8	2	6	1	3	4

Test 33
21 squares